The Mercy Marcy Foundation Journal

By Tina McClure

Exulon ELITE

www.xulonpress.com

DEDICATION

TO MY GRANDDAUGHTERS

ALLY
TIFFANY
KENDALL
DANI

I am blessed beyond measure
to have each of you in my life.

I LOVE YOU!

Ask GOD to direct your path
as you come out of your shadow
to pursue the dream that has been placed on your heart.

Pray, Believe and Receive!

# Marcy Mabel Marigold

My name is Marcy Mabel Marigold.

I am 12 years old. I NEVER use my middle name. UGH! Mom says she chose it because it means "Lovable"! It's strange that whenever she's irritated with me about something, she calls me Mabel! Weird! I guess it's a mom thing.

I love animals! Every one of them!

They love us no matter what and they need us to protect them from danger, starvation and homelessness. All they want is to be cared for just like you and me.

I am so lucky because my Mom and Dad understand me. They agree that GOD has given me the "Gift of Mercy."

My Dad calls me "MERCY MARCY."

Whenever I come through the door with a new friend who needs help, he looks at me, rolls his eyes up and then gives me a big smile! It never fails, we both start cracking up!

Tonight, at dinner, I was telling them about my idea for a place to keep the animals I find until I can get them the right home. It has to be a safe place and room enough for supplies too. They loved this idea!

Mom said, "Marcy, I can tell you have a BIG dream right now!" I told her that I want to help as many animals as I can.

Dad was deep in thought and I asked him what he was thinking about. "Marcy, I now know how Noah must have felt when GOD chose him to build the Ark."

Mom is an environmentalist, and she would be very unhappy if Dad had to cut any of the trees down. She loves nature and things that look natural. Dad knew he had to come up with an idea that would not only work for the animals, but please both of his girls too. When he said he was going outside, I jumped up from the table like a hyper head!

I wanted to go with him, when Mom said, "MABEL", your friends, the dishes, are waiting for you!" Oh great! Dad looked at me and said, "I think you'd better listen to your mother, she sounds serious! I will have a surprise for you tomorrow after school."

I gave him a big hug and thanked him.

Every night when I'm through saying my prayers, I choose a word that I like to give a special meaning to my day.

My word for today is:
Grateful

🐦 The Big Surprise

Today, I went on a field trip with the Photography Club to the Nature Center. It was awesome! I love taking pictures of animals and people! Another thing I really like to do is cut out silhouettes of all kinds of things, especially, animals! Silhouettes remind me of shadows, and what's really cool is that we all have one.

I was so excited to get home from school today. Good thing I went on the field trip. I don't think I could have sat at my desk all day and concentrated on anything. Mom was in the kitchen. There were fresh vegetables from her garden on the counter to be washed and she was going through

things to be recycled. When she saw me, she had a big smile on her face. You know, like she was keeping a big secret or something. I said, "WHAT?" She really started laughing then! "Dad has a surprise for you and he told me to send you to the back yard when you get home." I ran through the door and didn't stop until; Oh my!, I couldn't believe my eyes! Literally, I thought I was having an out of body experience! Dad had built a treehouse around a tree!

It was sealed at the top so nothing could come down the tree into the treehouse. There were birds and squirrels at the top of the tree looking down. So Cool! I asked him where in the world he came up with the idea. He told me that he and GOD worked it out. He said he started putting things together and everything fell into to place like a puzzle. WOW! He's not just a cool Dad, but a Genius!

I went inside the door and there were places for animals, crates, food, and all the supplies we would need. He had lights all around, inside and outside and he even put a little refrigerator inside in case we needed it. This is a dream come true. I never felt this way before. It's amazing!

My head was about to burst with ideas. We need a sign to put on the door. It will say;

The Mercy Marcy Foundation!

Mom said I needed to think of a Mission Statement. I looked at her like, what is that! She read my mind, and said it is a promise or a pledge made to everyone about what we are here to do. I thought about it and came up with:

"The Mercy Marcy Foundation promises to treat all animals with love and respect. We are here to give them all they need to be protected from harm, while we try to connect them with the right people who will love them."

Mom said she liked it and then she handed me a JOURNAL. It was a perfect size and had so many pages. She said to enjoy writing about experiences I have while I am trying to help animals and people. A great idea!

My word for today is:
Blessed

The Shadow

At school today, I met a new girl named Scarlett. She laughed and told me her parents call her "Star." When she was a baby, they said her eyes sparkled like little stars. I said, "Yep," sounds like another mom thing! She told me she moved here a couple of weeks ago and hasn't made any friends yet. She said it's hard when you come into a new school after it's already started. It also doesn't help when you are a little shy.

Scarlett opened her locker and on the door was the silhouette of a dog. I loved it! I asked her where she got it and she said she made it. She said making silhouettes is a

hobby of hers. WOW! It didn't take us long to become friends!

I asked her about her dog and she told me he was a rescue, a mixed breed, with the whitest, silkiest hair and the sweetest boy in the world. She had him about a week before she gave him a name because she wanted to see what his personality was like.

Every time she moved, he would follow her. He would be right on her heels as if they were attached to each other. She started laughing and said if she tried to tiptoe away from him while he was asleep, it never failed, he would wake up and start following her.

The rescue people said he was very insecure because he had been left alone in

an abandoned house with no food or water. He was very scared. I can't imagine how anyone could do this to an animal.

She said the way she named him was weird. She was outside raking up leaves for her Dad one day when her Mom called her to come in the house. The dog was laying in the grass watching her and she said, "let's go SHADOW!"

He got up and followed her to the house. It just seemed to fit. Her Mom called this a revelation! Some things just happen the way they are meant to.

I had so much on my mind when I left Scarlett. Everywhere I looked, I saw shadows. Then, I was watching my own shadow.

I am so excited about the Mercy Marcy Foundation. I just knew I had to make a difference for the animals and the people who loved them but it was all a little scary. How was I going to do it? I talked to my Dad about it and he reminded me to pray, have faith, and be patient.

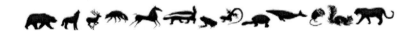

I woke up the next morning feeling happy. I knew what I had to do. I had to;

"Step Out Of My Shadow And Bring Love And Rescue To All Animals."

That was the answer!

My word for today is:
Faithful

🐈 The Three Kittens

I went for a walk with Dad today. It was chilly, and I was glad I wore my coat with big pockets so I could keep my hands warm. Dad saw a friend and they began talking. While I waited, I heard crying. I walked up the hill towards the sound. It was coming from behind a dumpster. There was a small orange tabby kitten huddled up in a patch of clover. She was scared and cold. I picked her up, gave her a hug, and put her in one of my coat pockets. While I turned to walk away, I heard another cry. I couldn't believe it! That cry came from the far side of the dumpster. I had to walk around some ferns to get to the sound. Under one of the big

ferns, I saw a small black kitten. Poor little thing was so shy. I picked her up and cuddled her a minute before I put her in my other pocket.

I started down the hill towards Dad, when I heard more crying. No way! The sound came from an old shed covered with ivy. When I tried to open the door, the ivy was wound around it so tight, I was having trouble pulling it open. I was pulling ivy in all directions and I started tugging on the door as hard as I could. Finally, it popped open. I was able to pick up a little gray kitten with black stripes who had the prettiest green eyes I've ever seen. This baby didn't really want a hug. She kept looking at me like, "It sure took you long enough!"

Totally an attitude thing! I was just laughing at her while I stuck her inside my coat.

I headed back towards Dad and fortunately I heard no more crying. I was wondering where the mom was. Dad's mouth dropped open, literally, and he said "What's this Marcy?" I laughed and said, "Dad, they are called kittens," then we both started laughing! I pulled the little orange kitten out of my pocket and told Dad I decided to name her CLOVER, then he held her while I got the little black kitten out of the other pocket. "This one's name is FERN," and then I reached inside my coat and pulled out number three. "This is IVY." Dad was commenting about those big green eyes. He asked me what I planned to do with them. I told him we need to have them checked out at the vet and they will tell us how to take care of them. When they get a little older, we can find a good home for them.

When we got to the vet, the attendant was very interested in the rescue story, and she loved the names. I explained to her that the names were appropriate because of where I found each one of them. Dad chimed in and said, "Marcy, your Mom is really going to love that! " I was smiling to myself. Mom will want me to show her where the ivy is so she can cut some to transplant in our yard. The attendant got a heating pad and asked me to put them all on it. I could tell they liked that. While I was petting each

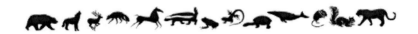

one, I could feel them purring. I told her we were going to have to find good homes for them. She said it would be a couple of weeks before they could be adopted because they still need to eat from a baby bottle. She figured someone just put them out because they didn't want them. Dad noticed in the waiting room that there was a list of people interested in adopting kittens and puppies. He wrote down some of the names and numbers.

We were about to leave, when the attendant said to come back in the morning if I wanted to feed the kittens their bottles. Dad smiled as he looked at the kittens and said, "Mercy Marcy will be here early in the morning."

I called the first number on the list Dad gave me when we got home. A woman said she and her husband would be interested in looking at the kittens. They would be there first thing tomorrow morning. They LOVE cats she said. (Keeping my fingers crossed!) After saying my prayers, I was thinking about how just an innocent walk can bring such a big responsibility. I'm so glad I was there today for those kittens.

Now this is what it's all about! I know some people do a lot to help animals, but there is no reason why everyone can't do just a little bit. It all makes a difference. Mom reminded me that after the kittens get adopted, I need to send a "Thank You" note to the vet and let them know how much I appreciated their help.

I think I will ask them if they would like to become a member of the Mercy Marcy Foundation too!

My word for today is:
Be Responsible

🦆 Waddles

The Mercy Marcy Foundation has been open for 2 days. I decided to ask people at school if they would like to become a member. The school counselor loved the idea and would be willing to place a sign-up sheet in her office for people to sign. Tomorrow morning she would make an announcement.

After school today, I went to the treehouse. There was a note on the door from my friend, Birdie. Her real name is Barbara, but because she loves anything with feathers, her family gave her the nickname. It's amazing how ducks, chickens and birds are never afraid around Birdie.

Her favorite hobbies are, of course, bird watching and making all kinds of bird sounds. She really does know how to communicate with them.

Her brother says she is, TOTALLY ANNOYING!

The note said, "Marcy, I have found a duck that needs our help!" I called her and told her I would meet her at the pond. I put some bread in my bag and jumped on my bike. I saw Birdie sitting by the pond with a little duck in her lap. She said two big ducks were trying to peck the little one and wouldn't let it in the water. The poor little thing went running in the bushes. Birdie tried to get it out, but the thorns in the bush were hurting her hands. The next thing she did was so cool! Birdie started making quacking noises and the little duck came right to her. I handed her the bread. WOW, that was a big hit. The little duck ate every bite. Birdie started walking in a big circle and saying, come on WADDLES, and the little duck followed her. It was amazing to watch. I loved it when Birdie would walk fast and then slow down to a slower pace and the little duck would copy her. Birdie and I started laughing. I told her I loved the name she came up with too.

Birdie told me she was really worried about Waddles. She needed to do something to help him. I told her to meet me at the tree house with Waddles in 30 minutes.

I rode to my next door neighbor's house as fast as I could. They were having a garage sale and this morning they had a plastic swimming pool in the yard. I jumped off my bike and saw Ben coming towards me. I told him the story and he asked his mom if she would donate the pool to The Mercy Marcy Foundation. She said she was happy to help out. Ben carried it over and put it near the treehouse. He was filling it up with water when we saw Birdie and Waddles making noises as they walked towards us. We were laughing our heads off. Ben said, "Birdie is a HOOT!" I was about to roll over on the ground laughing, and I said………"YEP, she loves Owls too"!

We put Waddles in the pool and he had so much fun swimming from one end of the pool to the other. Then he started turning upside down with his feet sticking straight up in the air. What a little showoff!

Ben wanted to be a member. I told him about the sign-up sheet at school and that the counselor was excited too. Mom came over to see Waddles and to say hello to Birdie and Ben. Ben said we need to figure

out a way to make money so we could buy the supplies for the treehouse. Mom said we could pick the gourds in her garden and make birdhouses out of them. The new members could paint them different colors and we could sell them. Ben loved the idea! Of course, he loved anything my mom said. She let him plant peanuts in her garden, then, using those peanuts, his mother would make the best homemade peanut butter. He plans to sell her peanut butter and save up for a new lawnmower because he wants to start his own lawn cutting business.

Birdie told us she would help. When she saw how happy Waddles was, she wanted to do whatever she could to help us. She said she knew her mom would buy several of the

birdhouses because they only had about 20 in their yard right now!

If it was up to Birdie, the whole yard would be covered in birdhouses, all shapes and sizes. She told us that one day, when she has her own house, she wants it to look like a big birdhouse. Ben was laughing until his side hurt. He said, "I can't wait to see that, Birdie!"

What a day.....a great day!

My two words for today are:
Concerned and Available

 A Whopper of a Day

While I was feeding the kittens at the vet today, the couple came by to see them. They loved the story about their rescue and thought the names were great. Since they couldn't make a decision, they decided to adopt all three! What a blessing, I am so happy they can all be together!

When I got to school, my teacher handed me a note from the Counselor. She has the sign-up sheet to give me today. WOW! I couldn't believe it! 32 people already signed up to be a member. She told me she put her name on the list too. She would also keep a new list in her office for more people to sign up.

When I got home from school, I saw Ben out in his yard. He got his new lawnmower and has 3 new customers. He said things were looking good. I told him about the new members and he smiled from ear to ear. He told me about his idea to have a Grand Opening. He said with that many members, there would be a great turn out. Everybody could put a sign up in their front yards and it would say:

GRAND OPENING
Mercy Marcy Foundation
Join us for FUN and Refreshments
2:00 p.m. to 5:00 p.m.
Everyone is Welcome!

Ben is so smart! What a genius of an idea! He's a Boy Scout and loves working on projects with other people. He's also a good organizer. We split up the new members list and called everyone to let them know. We told each person what to bring so there would be plenty of food. This was Ben's idea too! I still have my old lemonade stand. I will ask Mom to make her famous lemonade.

I called my friend, Ritchie. He said he would make the signs for us. He's a great artist and likes to paint all types of things. I told him he needed to bring some of his pet paintings to the Grand Opening so people can see how awesome they are.

I found Mom and Dad in the garden picking vegetables. I told them all the news and they thought everything sounded awesome.

They said to let them know what they could do, they would love to help. I laughed and said, "I'm sure I can think of SOMETHING!"

I headed to the treehouse to put Waddles in the pool for a little while. When I got closer, I couldn't believe my eyes. Oh my goodness, there were two new ducks in the pool. I was trying to figure out what to do because I didn't want them to be mean to Waddles. I heard somebody calling me and turned to see Birdie coming. Talk about a gift......that girl is amazing! She picked up the ducks, one at a time, and was talking to them. Then she put them back in the water and they were very still watching her. She told me to put Waddles in there with them while she was making duck noises. Now this was a sight to see. If I told somebody about this they would think I was looney tunes! She stepped back, made a couple of more duck noises and all of a sudden Waddles was showing off again. In a minute the other two ducks were copying him. Now all three were swimming to the left, then to the right and then, at the same time, they turned upside down and had their feet sticking straight up in the air!

Birdie and I were cracking up! She asked me if I knew who the ROCKETTES were. I said, "of course". She said, "well, these are the DUCKETTES!"

I thanked Birdie for all her help and she said she was glad it all worked out. I said to her, of course it did, that's why we call you, "Birdie!" She told me she was going to name the two new ducks, "PIDDLE" and "PADDLE"!

My word for the day is: Confident

The Grand Opening

Everything looked GREAT! Birdie's dad put up some speakers so we could hear the music and all the new members started singing, dancing and acting like they were on stage. It was so cool! Visitors were showing up and talked about how amazing the tree house was. They also loved the show that Waddles, Piddle and Paddle put on. The more people laughed at them, the crazier they acted!

Dad showed up carrying a big cardboard box. He asked me to get all the members together in front of the tree house. He told us how important each one of us was in making this Grand Opening a huge success.

He knew we were going to do many great things for animals and people. He opened the box and took out special T Shirts for all of us that said, "Proud Member of the Mercy Marcy Foundation" Of course, they were green, my Dad's favorite color. He reminded us of the "Golden Rule."

**"Do Unto Others As You
Would Have Them Do Unto You"**

He told us this rule applies to animals too. Everyone cheered and Dad took a group picture. I was thinking about how awesome it feels to belong to something with people who love the same things you do.

Visitors donated food, crates, toys, treats, blankets, bowls and anything they thought we could use. Some people left

money. Ben said we needed to vote on someone to be the treasurer. I told him that would be hard because some of us didn't know each other very well yet. So! Guess who the treasurer is? Right, Ben! Makes sense to me, he's great in math.

Birdie was talking "bird talk" to the ducks and people were cracking up. A couple came up to her and offered to take Waddles, Piddle and Paddle to live with them. They had a pond by their house and the ducks would love it. Birdie and I gave each other a hug because we knew those little ducks were going to have a great life. The couple told us to come over anytime to visit with them. Everybody helped clean up before they left. I love my new friends!

When I got back to the house, I found a note from my parents. They had to leave and wanted me to get my chores done. Not my favorite thing. I hear my Dad's voice in my head reminding me, "we are a family we have to help each other."

After I finished, the phone rang and it was a neighbor down the street. She told me there was a hawk flying around something in her back yard. She was scared to go see what it was. She didn't like the hawk so she wanted me to come over. Well, I'm certainly not afraid of a hawk, so I told her I was on my way. I couldn't believe it. A little puppy. It was so small, about as big as my hand. It was black and looked just like a little bear. I asked her if she had a small blanket I could wrap him up in and I carried him to the tree house.

Poor little thing. I wonder if the hawk dropped him. It seemed strange to me he was all alone. I was thinking, where was the mother and maybe more babies? I guess I will never know. I pulled out one of the carrier's someone donated today and a box

of puppy formula and a bottle that one of the new members brought. I mixed up the formula and he started drinking. He drank every bit of it and then let out a little burp! Yep, I knew I was in love. I will take him to the vet tomorrow to be checked out. I also need to make sure I am taking care of him properly because he's so tiny. I put him in the carrier and took him home.

Mom and Dad came home and I introduced him to them. I couldn't believe that Mom said the same thing I did about him looking like a little bear. They both wanted to hold him and Dad told me he would take me to the vet tomorrow.

Before I went to bed, I decided to feed him a little more formula. Mom came in and

I could tell she really liked him. I asked her if she and Dad would let me keep him. I told her I felt like his mommy and I was totally in love with him. Mom smiled that sneaky smile and said they knew this was going to happen. After all, she said, we are dealing with Marcy Mabel Marigold! She asked me if I had thought of a name. I told her it would be "Little Bear!" We both started laughing and then broke the news to dad.

I got in bed with Little Bear laying in his crate next to my bed. I thanked GOD for this amazing day and the many blessings.

My word for the day is: Committed

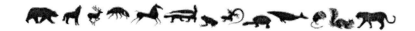

A Red Letter Day

Mom and Dad were in the kitchen. Little Bear and I were starving so I fixed my cereal and watched him gulp down his food. Yep! You always know when he's done because you hear the big BURP! Dad was leaving for work and Mom started washing the peaches she had picked from the tree. I was excited to hear she was going to make fresh peach ice cream. YUMMY, my favorite! I told her I was headed to the tree house to check on a few things because there was a members meeting at 4:00 today.

I saw the feral cat sitting behind the bushes when I got to the treehouse. Her food bowl was empty so I refilled it and gave her

fresh water. She must be going to have kittens because she's really getting fat.

Little Bear was looking at me with those pleading eyes, saying, "WALK!" I put on his leash and we headed to the neighborhood park where kids were playing. I saw a couple of my friends and they came along for the walk. Little Bear was really liking all the attention.

I mentioned I had been trying to keep him from licking everybody who showed him attention but it's not working to well. A couple of the boys thought this was cool so they started playing with him just to see what he would do. Someone actually left a sign at the treehouse the other day that said, "BEWARE, DOG CANNOT CONTROL HIS LICKER!" Do you think Little Bear really cares?

When I returned home, the letter carrier was delivering mail on my street. Her name is Katherine but people call her Miss Kat. I waited for her so I could say hello. She loves animals too and tells stories about lost and hurt animals she has helped. She has three cats who she talks about all the time. I asked

Miss Kat if she would like to be a member and she said she would love to. Even though she is older, she has the same heart for the animals as the rest of us. Age really doesn't matter when people have things in common. I invited her to come see the feral cat and she said she would stop by after work. She handed me the mail, and said it looked like I got a letter today.

I ran in the house and opened the envelope. It said:

Dear Marcy Marigold,

The City wants to invite you and your members to participate in the annual Fourth of July Parade. Please contact our office and let us know if you will be making a float for the parade or if you would prefer to walk. The parade will begin at 10:00 a.m. Sincerely, PARADE COORDINATOR City Hall

I couldn't believe it! I told Mom and she was over the top excited! She said, Dad works with a man who has a truck. Maybe he will let you borrow it. Dad could drive it in the parade.

Birdie came by with a baby bird that had fallen out of a nest.

We knew it was going to need more help than we could give it, so her mom offered to take us to the Nature Center. They said

they would keep it and care for it until they could let it go.

I told Birdie and her Mom about the parade. They were like Mom, over the top excited!

Birdie's Mom told me she had some extra crepe paper and poster paper she would give us to decorate with. She would talk to some of her friends to see if they had anything we could use.

Just as I thought, the members were, YES, over the top excited too! They liked the idea of riding in the truck, but now that our membership has grown to 51 people, it wouldn't hold us all. Different members had different ideas, but the best one, we all agreed to, was that we would take turns

riding. The riders would be holding the posters. The walkers would walk and anyone who wanted to bring their dog, could. Then, we had a drawing to see who would wear red, white or blue t shirts that day. We thought mixing them up would be more festive. We made a note to buy some candy out of our savings to throw to the kids.

Miss Kat was able to make the meeting, so when everyone left, I took her to see the feral cat. Yep, she said. She's definitely going to have kittens.

I told her the Vet keeps a list of people who want to adopt puppies or kittens and we will contact them when the babies are born. Miss Kat said the mama cat would have to feed her babies at least 6 weeks

before we do that. I'm remembering the three kittens I found and how they had to take a bottle because they had no mama.

I saw Dad walking up the driveway. Miss Kat and I said goodbye to each other and I ran to tell Dad about the parade. Before I could ask, he said he would talk to his friend about us borrowing the truck again. Two great minds thinking about the same thing at once, I said.

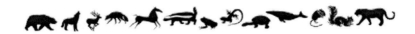

We both started laughing and he said, "we might have to have a "decorate the truck" cookout at the treehouse before the parade." The man is always thinking! I'm loving all his ideas!

Today was a great day. I am so lucky to have such special people in my life.

My word for today is: Humble

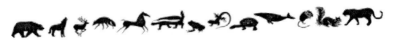

Sparkles and Fireworks

Today is the BIG day!! The truck looks great with all the posters, crepe paper, flags and balloons. Dad took a picture of all the members and had it blown up poster size. We attached it to the back of the truck. Of course, everybody wore their festive bandana and t-shirts. We all made paper hats with a flag stuck in it. I put a bandana on Little Bear and he let me know in a hurry he wasn't going to wear a t-shirt!

It was almost time for the parade to begin. The music started playing and everyone was moving around. The first group of members got in the truck with the animal posters. All the walkers were behind

the truck and some were walking their dog, others were throwing candy. Dad was driving and Little Bear sat next to him on the passenger seat.

When we reached the end of the parade, there were people cooking hot dogs, hamburgers, and ribs. There was watermelon, potato salad, coleslaw, baked beans and so many cakes, cookies, pies and an assortment of drinks.

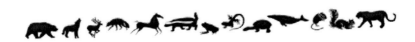

After lunch, there were games to play. Many people were throwing Frisbees to their dogs. Others were playing horseshoes. Dads and boys were playing softball, while many women were participating in the cake walks.

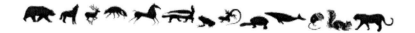

There was a local band playing music while teenagers were dancing and little kids were copying them. Some older people were making up their own dances to the music. Now that was really a sight! One man was dancing with his walking cane like it was his partner. People were laughing and having a great time.

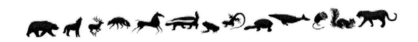

All the members walked around passing out pamphlets and answering questions about The Mercy Marcy Foundation. It was interesting to hear some of the animal stories people had to share.

While I was handing out pamphlets, I met some people who worked at one of the rescue shelters in town. It was interesting to hear what all they try to do for the animals when they get them. I learned they were a "no kill shelter," which means they keep the animals until they can place them with a good family. They said they were lucky because they had some good volunteers and many donations. The reason there were "kill shelters" was because they didn't have enough donations or volunteers to be able to

do that. I needed to talk to Ben about this. We can make a difference here.

I'm remembering again, some people do a lot, but everybody can do something!

A couple came up to me and asked if we ever do any pet sitting. "Hmm! Never thought of that," I said. They gave me their number and asked me to call if we ever do. I was thinking how amazing that would be.

All of us at The Mercy Marcy Foundation could help each other with the pet sitting; then the people would pay us a fee for our service; we could donate the money to the rescue shelters; then they can buy more supplies; we could even volunteer our services there too and that way there would be no more "kill shelters"! This helps everybody, and especially the animals.

Oh my goodness! Look at the people and animals who will be able to come out of their shadows! We need to have a meeting about this right away! Just think, we already have our first client!

You never know what will happen next!

My words for today are:
Committed and Focused

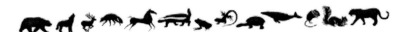

Bibbity, Bobbity, Boo

Today is Halloween! Everyone has been working hard to make our first Halloween Party a "SPOOKTACULAR" success. The first thing we will do is have the costume contest. All the costumes have to be made from things we find at home. That will be so much fun because nobody will look like anybody else.

I'm going to dress up in one of my mom's fancy dresses, a pair of her high heel shoes, make-up, curls in my hair and wear the big hat that hangs in the attic. Mom said her Aunt Martha gave it to her before she and Dad got married. I guess that would make it an antique? The final touch will be a pair

of clip on shades which will go over some pretend glasses I have.

Birdie called me and wanted me to come over and help her make some wings out of her mom's feather duster. Of course, she is going to be a bird!

She is going to wear her black leotards with some green tights that she painted red

stripes on. She will make a beak out of construction paper and tie it to the back of her head.

We both started laughing just thinking about it. Believe me, if you ever met Birdie, you would never forget her!

The moms started bringing the cool food to the tree house and setting it out on the tables. They had made Ghost Sandwiches, Eye ball Salad, Mummy Dogs, Pumpkin Krispies, Boo Burgers, Skeleton Hands, (some kind of cream cheese something or other), Pumpkin Ice Cream Sandwiches, and of course, French Fries. They made a really cool orange punch too.

Dad picked the biggest pumpkin he could find in the garden. He had a pair of his old

jeans, a plaid shirt and an old straw hat. I grabbed some newspapers out of the recycle bin and took them to him. We started stuffing the pumpkin's clothes and then painted the face with the biggest smile you have ever seen.

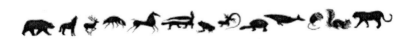

Dad decided he wanted to paint one eye closed so it would look like the pumpkin man was winking and then he sat him on top of some bails of straw next to the treehouse door.

Someone put the music on and everybody started dancing to the Monster Mash. This was really fun because the adults were acting so weird! When it was time for the costume contest, we had to line up, and all of sudden a person dressed up like a very scary witch stood in front of us. She made the scary witch laughing noise and said, "Come, you little chickadees, let's get started!" We were all looking back and forth at each other trying to figure out who that was. We knew it was a female because she had a high pitched voice. The costumes were awesome and everyone looked amazing! I would really have a hard time choosing someone.

The witch made her decision and, of course, Birdie took the prize! We all thought she should get it. The witch started that scary laugh again, but, then, made the mistake of saying something in her normal voice. I started laughing and yelled out, that's Miss Kat! She took off her mask and we were all cracking up

It was time to start cleaning up so we all pitched in. Someone called out at the top of their voice that a little dog was running back and forth in front of the tree house. It was a puppy and it looked lost. He was

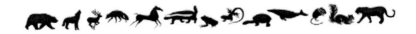

barking like crazy and there was no tag on him. We didn't even know which way he came from. I ran down and gave him water and put him in a crate for now so he would be safe.

We would have to put up signs to see if anyone is missing him.

Little Bear hopes we don't find out who he belongs to. Today was so much fun.

My word for today is: Thankful!

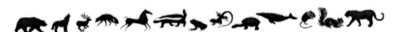

A Major Moment

When I got home, Ben came over to see if I wanted to ride bikes to the place where the boy scouts were going to camp out next weekend. He saw Dad and invited him too!

We had so much fun passing each other on the dirt road that led us to the camp site. Ben walked around picking up sticks, rocks and other sharp objects. There was a big hill over on the other side so we decided to check it out. When we reached the top, we saw the road, and then, we saw a dog and he was moaning. We ran as fast as we could and realized he had been hit by a car and just left there. Dad and Ben took off their shirts and laid them on the dog to keep him warm. Dad said we needed to get him to the vet immediately. He took out his cell phone and called the police. He told them the situation and that we were on bikes. They said they would send a police car right away.

I was looking at the dog and his eyes showed me he was in pain. I couldn't help it, I started crying. How could anybody do this?

Ben tried to make me feel better by reminding me that we can't make everybody else do the right thing, but at least we can.

I said a silent prayer for the poor little dog.

Dad told me the Mercy Marcy Foundation could help by informing people about what to do in this kind of emergency. I was holding the dog's paw. It seemed to make him stop shaking some. The police pulled up in a van instead of a regular police car. They took out something called a gurney and laid it on the ground next to the

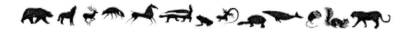

dog. Dad helped them to gently move the dog on top of it. They laid him in the back of the van, and made sure it was secure so it wouldn't move. My heart felt so heavy for that poor little fellow.

By the time we got to the vet, he had been carried to a special room to be examined. I asked the receptionist if I could just hold his paw and tell him a secret before the doctor came in. She took me to his room and he was just lying there so still. I walked in front of him so he could see me. His eyes were closed, but when I picked up his paw, he opened them and looked at me right in the eyes. I told him that I loved him and I was sorry this happened to him. I thought he was very brave. I promised him I wouldn't leave him and I was going to say a special prayer for him. I knew he was in pain and I didn't want him to be. So I prayed.

I knew GOD loved him too.

I heard Dad's voice in my mind reminding me that;

Not only does GOD have a plan for people, but HE has a plan for animals too.

Whatever happens to him, we need to remember that his life is special too.

The doctor came in and while he was telling us about the many injuries, the dog took a deep breath and passed away.

I was a mess!

I looked down and I was still holding his paw. The doctor put his arm over my shoulder and said I needed to remember that he's no longer in pain. He had so many internal injuries, we could not have saved him.

I moved my hand from his paw and looked up at Dad and Ben.

The Mercy Marcy Foundation Journal

I could tell Ben was holding back his tears. Dad put his arm around me and said, "Marcy, that dog has left you a gift. He wants you to use his life as an example. We all need to be responsible. Where there's a will there's a way to help people and animals in every situation. We should never walk away! He has given you a major lesson to teach. Remember, he is with GOD now and happy.

He trusts you to teach others.

When we got home all I wanted to do was go to my room. I had to think about what Dad said. I said another prayer for the dog and asked GOD to let him know I love him. I was thinking I don't think I have ever felt

so sad and I realized I didn't even know his name. I just know that something felt different inside of me and I just wanted people to know that no living thing should ever be left alone to be in pain and die.

Ben and Dad were outside talking. I told them I felt like my heart grew a little bit bigger since this morning.

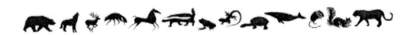

Ben said he was glad the dog was not in pain anymore. I told them I had given the dog a name. It is MAJOR. They both liked it. Dad said, "MAJOR definitely made an impact on the three of us.

His life had a legacy that will help others be more compassionate and loyal to each other and to all animals. I didn't know him long, but I will never forget him.

My words for today are:
Compassion and Responsible

"My Journal is not full, this is only the beginning. There are so many more stories to tell and a lot more animals to help"!

Mercy Marcy.

To Be Continued...

ABOUT THE AUTHOR

Tina McClure, a native of Atlanta, Georgia has been involved with animals and children all of her life. The oldest of 5 children, she got an early start. She is the mother of two children, a son and daughter, and four grandchildren.

 At 72, she is still going strong! She is the owner of YOUR PET'S NANNY, a service providing professional and loving pet care for all furry, feathered and finney friends. Midday Walks and In-home Care is available seven days a week, and a BED and BREAKFAST is available for a limited number of dogs, while clients are traveling.

It is not unusual to catch Tina preparing a special recipe for clients who are experiencing problems with their dogs eating habits. She calls it "DOGGY DELIGHT"! It has become so successful that many clients are asking for the recipe.

She hopes you will join Mercy Marcy on FACEBOOK. Share your stories with new friends while we work to make a difference for animals.

ACKNOWLEDGEMENTS

To the many rescue volunteers and foster families who give faithfully and lovingly to all God's creatures. You never know what you are going to get, but each one brings unconditional love.

> *"You work for a cause,*
> *Not for applause,*
> *Live life to express,*
> *Not to impress*
> *Don't strive to make your presence known,*
> *Just make your absence felt."*
>   Author unknown

I have enjoyed meeting and working with many of you. Also recognizing the many businesses, organizations, and individuals who always find new ways to make a difference through fundraising and other special events.

> *Proverbs 31:8*
> *"Speak up for those who cannot speak for themselves,*
> *for the rights of all who are destitute."*

I would like to acknowledge Gary Sanchez, Illustrator of this book. You have been a marvel to work with. Your professionalism, passion and faith have been attributes which make you shine. God bless you and your family for what you do for rescue animals.

I would also like to recognize Christopher Gill,
   www.fishbonephotos.com

CPSIA information can be obtained at www.ICGtesting.com
Printed in the USA
LVOW09s2336210215

427703LV00003B/130/P